undercover operations

Adam Sutherland

First published in 2012 by Wayland

Wayland
Hachette Children's Books
338 Euston Road
London NW1 3BH

Wayland Australia
Level 17/207 Kent Street
Sydney NSW 2000

Concept by Joyce Bentley

Commissioned by Debbie Foy
and Rasha Elsaeed

Produced for Wayland by Calcium
Designer: Paul Myerscough
Editor: Sarah Eason

Photographer: Meg Hawkins

British Library Cataloguing in Publication Data

Undercover operations. — (Police and
combat)(Radar)
1. Police patrol—Surveillance operations—
Juvenile literature. 2. Undercover operations—
Juvenile literature. 3. Criminal investigation—
Juvenile literature.
I. Series
363.2'32-dc22

ISBN: 978 0 7502 6592 8

Printed in China

Wayland is a division of Hachette Children's Books,
an Hachette UK company.

www.hachette.co.uk

Acknowledgements: Alamy: Photos 12 23; Dreamstime: Basphoto 2tl, 4–5, Hypestock 3br, 21b, Nicemonkey 22–23; Getty Images: 17; iStock: Andrew J Shearer 13, Vika Valter 18–19; Photos.com: cover; Shutterstock: Ryan Rodrick Beiler 6–7, Anthony Correia 15l, Fred Goldstein 10–11, Kheng Guan Toh 8–9, K2 Images 10br, Peter Kim 26br, Martin Muránsky 2tr, 20tr, P Cruciatti 20br, Rorem 27tr, Martin Spurny 1, Testing 15r, Jurgen Ziewe 21tr; Wikimedia: 16, 2br, 28–29, 14l, 14r, 11c, 28.

cover stories

thepeople

theskills

thetalk

KEEPING MY COUNTRY SAFE

MY STORY BY 'ALEX'

Interview courtesy of MI6

From an early age, I had always been drawn to the idea of working in intelligence, but never really knew how to go about getting into it.

After graduating from university with a degree in history and politics, I answered an advert for work in a government department with opportunities for foreign travel. It turned out to be a recruitment drive for the UK's Secret Intelligence Service (SIS), better known as MI6.

After an intensive training course, I joined a small team working on counter-narcotics. There was a real sense of achievement between us when things went to plan. We all wanted our colleagues to succeed, to gather secret intelligence and to return safely from their missions.

After that, I spent a couple of years in Afghanistan. I worked closely with the British military and various partners on counter-terrorism operations. This was definitely an experience of a lifetime: making a difference to people who really need it, and keeping our country safer.

On my return to London, I began my current role as a targeting officer working on terrorist threats to UK interests. I work closely with MI5, Government Communications Headquarters (GCHQ) and the police in an attempt to stop the threats becoming a terrorist attack. As a Londoner, and someone who took the underground on the morning of 7 July 2005 during the bombings, it isn't difficult to be inspired to come to work each day. Part of my role is to try to ensure that the intelligence we get will stop a terrorist plot.

Working for the SIS, you really do feel that you are making a difference. I regularly have moments where I stop and think 'I can't believe that I'm actually being paid to do this'. Not a lot of people can say that!

Protect and serve

The US Secret Service's main mission is to protect the country against financial and computer fraud, and money laundering – an important source of funds for many terrorist organisations. The Secret Service also protects the US president, and acts as his bodyguards both at home (such as during President Obama's inauguration, below) and on foreign visits.

TOP SECRET AGENCIES

Surveillance and intelligence gathering are both types of undercover operations carried out by specialised government agencies. The agencies are often referred to as 'secret services', because their duties are not well known...

SECURITY IN BRITAIN

The British Security Service, also known as Military Intelligence, Section 5 (MI5), is responsible for protecting its country against threats to national security. MI5 guards the UK against espionage attempts from other countries, terrorism and sabotage.

BRITISH SECURITY ABROAD

The Secret Intelligence Service (SIS), or Military Intelligence, Section 6 (MI6), collects Britain's foreign intelligence. It finds information on the plans of foreign governments or terrorist groups and seeks to disrupt terrorist activities.

ACTING ON INTELLIGENCE

In the US, the Central Intelligence Agency (CIA) collects information about foreign governments, companies or individuals, and passes that information to the US government. The CIA also conducts undercover operations and military missions.

DEFENDING THE US

The main goal of the Federal Bureau of Investigation (FBI) is to protect and defend the US against terrorist and foreign intelligence threats, and to uphold and enforce criminal laws. The FBI is increasingly involved in protecting important computer systems against cyber attacks.

STATS

20,000

The estimated number of CIA employees around the world.

16th CENTURY

The earliest recorded accounts of spies in the UK, who were working on behalf of King Henry VIII.

272,000

The number of secret files held by MI5 on 'suspicious individuals' in the UK. That's one in every 160 adults!

41

The percentage of female employees within MI5. It employs 3,800 people.

4.9

BILLION

The FBI's annual budget in British pounds (US$7.9 billion).

39

MILLION

The estimated number of spies in China – that's three per cent of its population!

30

The number of Russian spies believed to be based at the Russian Embassy in London, UK.

1,271

The estimated number of US government organisations working on counter-terrorism, homeland security and intelligence.

THE CIA

Like every secret service, the CIA has its own unique structure. This is how the US intelligence agency is organised to fight terrorism and keep the United States safe.

ACTING ON INTELLIGENCE

Officers in the CIA's Directorate of Intelligence (DI) are expected to assess fast-moving international developments and decide what effect they will have on the United States. DI officers produce reports such as the daily World Intelligence Review (WIRe). The WIRe is an electronic publication aimed at senior US government officials. The CIA analysis of overseas intelligence helps to keep government well informed of events that are going on around the world.

VERY IMPORTANT PEOPLE

The job of Human Resources (HR) is to hire the brightest talents, and to help them develop the skills needed to serve their country. The CIA's recruitment centre is constantly looking to hire highly qualified men and women from a wide range of ethnic and cultural backgrounds. It has struck up partnerships with several US colleges and universities, which are important sources of talent.

The Office of Public Affairs (OPA) ensured that President Obama was fully briefed before he told the nation that the mission to find Bin Laden had been successful.

UNDERCOVER OPERATIONS

The National Clandestine Service (NCS) is the CIA's undercover arm, which coordinates and monitors undercover operations across all the US intelligence agencies. With the aim of strengthening national security, the NCS collects information from its contacts around the world and briefs the US president and senior government officials on important discoveries.

INFORMING THE PUBLIC

The CIA communicates with the outside world through the OPA. The Director of OPA oversees all the CIA's dealings with the press, television and radio, and the public. While always protecting classified information, the OPA has made a large amount of information about the agency available to the public to try to provide openness and to encourage trust among US citizens.

TECHNICAL SUPPORT

The Directorate of Science and Technology (DS&T) creates the NCS computer systems and data analysis programmes. Workers come from fields of science, such as computer programming and engineering. They bring a range of different skills and specialisms to the job, from code-breaking through to designing new satellite surveillance techniques.

JAMES BOND

THE ULTIMATE SPY

THE BIRTH OF 007

James Bond was 'born' in 1952, created by the writer Ian Fleming. James's father, Andrew, was Scottish, his mother, Monique Delacroix, was Swiss. The young Bond spent his childhood travelling around Europe because of his father's work in the arms industry. As a result, James Bond speaks French and German fluently.

GROWING UP FAST

When James was just 11 years old, his parents were killed in a mountain climbing accident, and he moved back to England to live with an aunt, Miss Charmain Bond. He attended Eton College, one of Britain's most prestigious private schools, but was expelled for bad behaviour!

After university, Bond joined the Royal Navy and fought in World War II, rising to the rank of Commander.

SECRET SERVICE

While in the Navy, Bond joined the Special Boat Service (SBS) and was then placed in the 030 Special Forces Unit. He served undercover in Iraq, Iran and Libya, and fought in Bosnia. From the SBS, Bond was recruited by the Royal Naval Reserve (RNR) Defence Intelligence Group. He studied Oriental Languages, and came top of his class for physical endurance, logic and psychological operations. He served in the Navy from the ages of 17 to 31, joining MI6 at the age of 30.

LICENCE TO KILL

The two 00s in Bond's codename 007 refer to the two kills he made in the 1953 book, *Casino Royale,* to join the ranks of the senior MI6 agents. Bond favours the Walther PPK pistol although he is also an expert of close quarter combat and martial arts. He drives an Aston Martin DB5 and, when he is not on assignment, lives in a flat in Chelsea, London, and says his favourite food is scrambled eggs. An ordinary man, with an extraordinary job, James Bond is the most famous secret agent in history!

Career highlights

1953 first Bond novel published, *Casino Royale*

1962 first Bond film, *Dr No*, is released with actor Sean Connery playing James Bond

2006 original Aston Martin DB5 sold for £2.6 million ($4.2 million)

2012 twenty-third Bond film, as yet untitled, is scheduled for release on 9 November 2012

THE STATS

Name: James Bond
Born: 1952
Place of birth: Unknown
Height: 183 cm (6 ft)
Weight: 76 kg (167 lb)
Job: Intelligence officer for the British Secret Intelligence Service (MI6)

Daniel Craig took over the role of James Bond in 2006 in the film *Casino Royale* followed by *Quantum of Solace* in 2008.

GLOBAL INTELLIGENCE

Like the CIA and many other secret services, the BND and SVR have their own symbols (left and above).

Undercover operations and intelligence gathering are crucial parts of every nation's security planning. This means that each country has its own well-organised and well-funded secret service. Here are some of the best known.

EUROPEAN PROTECTION

Germany's foreign intelligence agency, the Bundesnachrichtendienst (BND), which means Federal Intelligence Service, acts as an early warning system to alert the German government to threats from abroad. Using wiretapping and electronic surveillance, the BND collects information on threats such as terrorism and organised crime. With 300 offices in Germany and around the world, the BND employs about 6,000 people (ten per cent are trained soldiers).

THE IRON CURTAIN

The Russian External Intelligence Service (SVR) is responsible for intelligence and espionage activities outside Russia. It advises the Russian president on security threats from abroad, and is authorised to negotiate anti-terrorist cooperation and intelligence-sharing arrangements with foreign agencies. During the Soviet era,

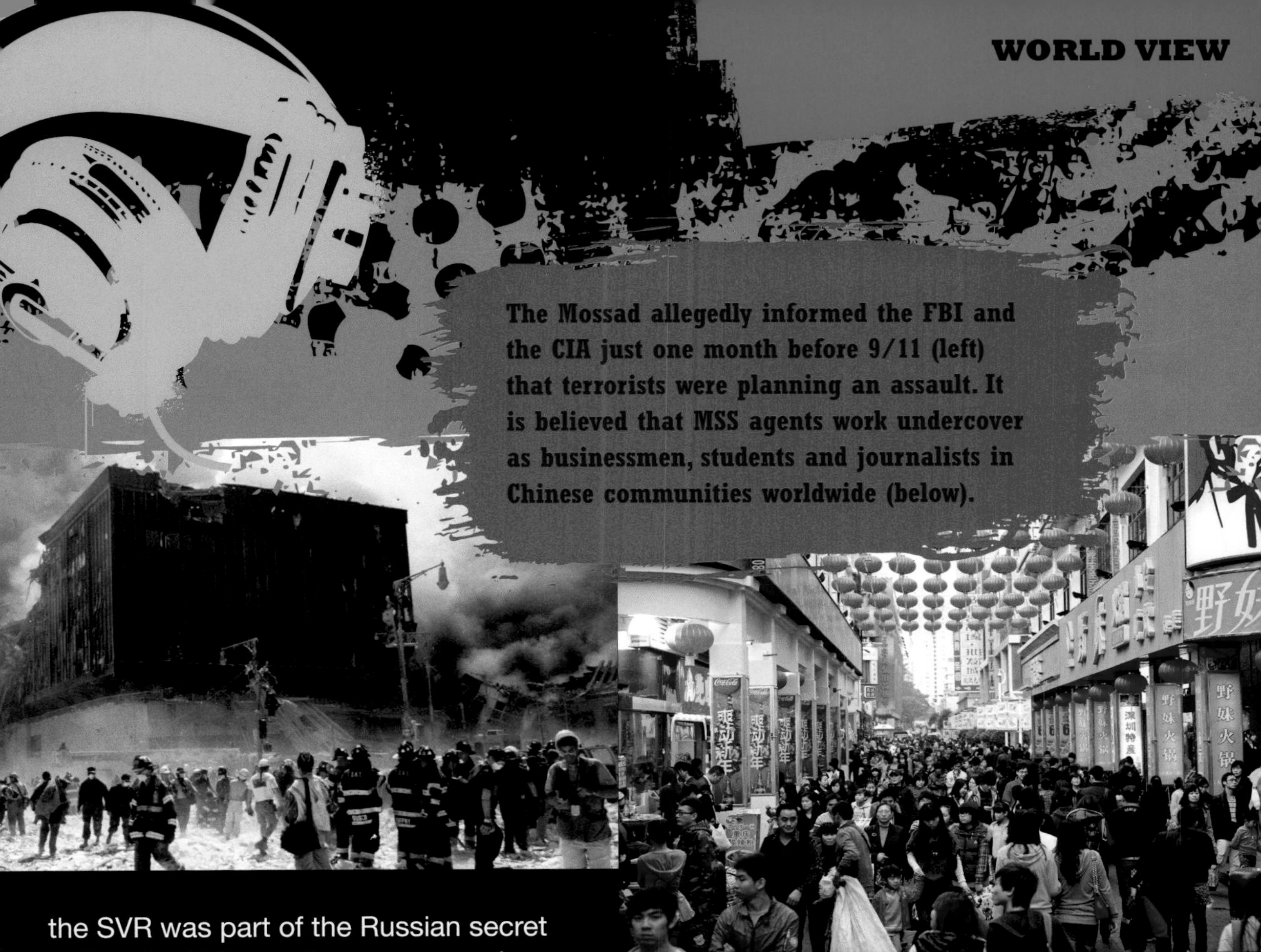

The Mossad allegedly informed the FBI and the CIA just one month before 9/11 (left) that terrorists were planning an assault. It is believed that MSS agents work undercover as businessmen, students and journalists in Chinese communities worldwide (below).

the SVR was part of the Russian secret police, the KGB, and was rumoured to handle foreign political assassinations.

FRANCE FIGHTS TERRORISM

The General Directorate for External Security (DGSE) is France's external intelligence agency. The agency works alongside the DCRI (Central Directorate of Interior Intelligence) to provide information and protect national security through counter-intelligence operations abroad. The DGSE may have prevented more than 15 terrorist attacks in France since the 11 September 2001 attacks (9/11).

THE HOLY LAND

The Mossad is Israel's national intelligence agency and is responsible for information gathering and undercover operations outside Israel's borders. Together with Aman (military intelligence) and Shin Bet (internal security), the Mossad makes up a vital part of Israel's intelligence network and community.

EASTERN INTELLIGENCE

The Ministry of State Security (MSS) is China's largest and most active foreign intelligence agency. One of its main roles is gathering foreign intelligence, and its agents are active all over the world, from Hong Kong and Taiwan to the USA and Europe. The Chinese government seeks intelligence from all parts of Chinese life, so employees are active in many areas including politics, business, industry and education.

THE STORY OF ESPIONAGE

Sir Francis Walsingham (1532–1590) was one of Elizabeth I's most trusted advisors – and a legendary spy.

Espionage, or spying, has been going on for thousands of years. As far back as 500 BCE, ancient Chinese and Indian military leaders wrote detailed studies on how to deceive their enemies. Hieroglyphs show spies operating in the ancient Egyptian court. Spies were used to uncover disloyal subjects and to locate tribes that could be conquered and enslaved.

ROMAN INTELLIGENCE

The Roman Empire's intelligence forces provided reports on the military strength of its enemies. The Roman military employed intelligence forces to infiltrate rebel tribes and convince leaders to join forces with Rome. In 44 BCE, Roman spies told Julius Caesar of the plot to kill him, but he chose to ignore the information and was killed by his enemies.

SPYING THROUGH THE AGES

In the sixteenth century, the English royal court developed the world's leading spy network. King Henry VIII created a large secret police force to locate groups loyal to the Church. His daughter, Elizabeth I, employed at least 50 secret agents in Britain and across Europe to discover plots to overthrow her. It was also at this time that secret codes, magnifying glasses and the first hidden cameras made spying easier to carry out.

REVOLUTIONARY ACTS

US president George Washington, and Founding Father Benjamin Franklin, both spied for their country against the British during the American Revolutionary War (1775-1783). Washington was an expert in military deception, and once tricked the British Army into believing he was about to attack New York City when his troops were actually in Yorktown, Virginia, 640 kilometres away!

EAST VERSUS WEST

The political tensions between the USA and Western democracies, and the Soviet Union and China that rapidly developed after World War II (1939–1945) provoked an intense period of spying on both sides. The 'Cold War', as it was known, saw a massive expansion in countries' nuclear weapons building programmes, and spies were employed to find and pass secrets to each side.

CIA director Leon Panetta (right) and his key aids informed Congress in person that Bin Laden had been killed.

Spying on terrorists

In the last 20 years, agencies have been more likely to target the illegal drug trade and the threat of terrorism than spy on old enemies in the East. The discovery of Osama Bin Laden's hide-out and information leading to the special forces raid, which resulted in his death, is believed to have been supplied by CIA informers.

UNDER SURVEILLANCE

You wait and listen for hours and hours, days and days. You sit in your hastily equipped, makeshift office that has been constructed to house you and your equipment, defending your country. Headphones cover your ears and you strain to pick out meaningful, important conversations. Even a few words can make a difference. The fate of thousands of people depends on what you alone hear.

ON WATCH

You've been tracking this target for months. All the intelligence points to him being linked with a group of extremists who are thought to be planning terrorist attacks. It is your team's job to locate him, track his movements and find a way of monitoring who he talks to and what he says.

COLLECTING EVIDENCE

The biggest challenge is getting a listening device into position. Terrorists know their mobile phones can be used to track their location and monitor their conversations, but some are more careful than others. You discovered their headquarters three months ago, thanks to a conversation between two younger recruits to the group. After that, it was a case of working out how to get a microphone in there. But you did it and it's proving invaluable.

READY TO ACT!

Suddenly you hear something important. Your heart starts to thud like a drum as you realise the significance of the words. The hairs on the back of your neck stand up, but you must stay calm. This could be the breakthrough you've been waiting for – the chance to pass this information back to head office and let them plan the next move. You could be the key to putting these terrorists behind bars! You feel exhilarated and a small thrill rips through you like a jolt of electricity. You feel proud to be keeping your country safe.

YOU ARE NOT ALONE!

Undercover organisations have developed several ingenious methods to track their targets. Here are their key surveillance techniques.

WATCHING THE WEB

Organisations such as the FBI spend millions of dollars monitoring internet traffic. People who visit certain websites or use particular 'trigger' words can be picked out by computer programmes and flagged up for closer inspection.

STREET CORNER CAMERAS

In the UK, there are more than 4.2 million surveillance cameras (also known as CCTV) – one camera for every 15 people! China now plans to build a database that will track the movements of its 1.3 billion people.

SOCIAL SPY NETWORKS

The information that suspected criminals leave on social networking sites such as Facebook and Twitter can be used to extract useful information about them.

EYES IN THE SKY

The UK police force plans to use unmanned aerial vehicles (UAVs) to keep a constant watch on crime. In the US, UAVs are used to patrol the American-Mexican border to watch out for illegal immigrants.

MOBILE PHONES

Two of the USA's largest phone companies – AT&T and Verizon – are paid over a million dollars every year by the FBI to be able to search the records of all the phone calls made on their lines.

CCTV is used for general security and for traffic offences, but it is also increasingly used for surveillance by undercover organisations.

Some governments in the world are allowed to monitor all internet activity.

UAV cameras are so sensitive that they can sense the heat of a human body from 60 kilometres away.

Most mobile phone surveillance is used to track the whereabouts of the phone user.

The glamorous and dangerous world of espionage is often portrayed in popular culture.

BOND, JAMES BOND

James Bond is probably the world's most famous spy. The fictional MI6 agent has appeared in a total of 13 titles, including *Live and Let Die*, *The Spy Who Loved Me* and *Moonraker*. Since Bond made his first appearance on the big screen in the 1962 film *Dr No*, the Bond films have grossed over £3 billion worldwide at the box office!

IMPOSSIBLE HIT

Hollywood superstar Tom Cruise is the star of the *Mission: Impossible* films, which first hit cinemas in 1996. Cruise plays agent Ethan Hunt, who leads an Impossible Missions Force, an unofficial branch of the CIA. *Mission: Impossible* started life as a popular 1960s US TV series.

TEENAGE SPY!

Teen orphan Alex Rider stars in the *Stormbreaker* series of books, by Anthony Horowitz. The first novel was published in 2000, and has been followed by a further eight titles, with more in the pipeline. The series follows Rider through his thrilling MI6 missions, an organisation he joins when his uncle is killed in action. A *Stormbreaker* movie was released in 2006, and a TV series is on the way!

SECRET IDENTITY

Ex-CIA agent Jason Bourne is another character that started in books and has become a success on the big screen. Writer Robert Ludlum wrote the first Bourne novel, *The Bourne Identity*, in 1980. Jason Bourne is a highly-trained undercover killer with no memory of his past life, fighting to regain his identity. Ludlum's first three books became a series of hit movies, with actor Matt Damon playing the mysterious agent Bourne.

***The Bourne Identity*, *The Bourne Supremacy* and *The Bourne Ultimatum*, have taken more than £600 million (US$976 million) at the box office.**

INVISIBLE INK

Do you want to create top-secret messages that only your friends will be able to read? Here's how!

You will need:

- juice of 1 lemon • bowl
- plain paper • paintbrush
- heat source, such as a lamp or sunlight

1

Squeeze some lemon juice into a bowl.

2

Using the juice as 'ink', take a paintbrush and write a message onto a piece of paper.

3

Allow the paper to dry – the message will become invisible.

4

To read the invisible message, hold the paper to the heat source. If necessary, ask an adult to help you.

5

Lemon juice is mildly acidic and weakens paper. When the paper is heated, the acid turns the writing dark, so the message can now be read.

Got it?

Another way to read the message is to put salt on the drying 'ink'. After a minute, wipe off the salt and colour over the paper with a wax crayon. Your message will appear!

SPY CHATTER

Break the spy speak code with Radar's stealthy guide!

anti-tank missile
a missile designed to pierce a tank's armour plating

codename
a secret name that is designed to protect a person's identity

counter-intelligence
activities designed to stop or attempt to stop enemy spying

counter-narcotics
operations to prevent the growing, transportation and selling of drugs

counter-terrorism
the methods that governments use to prevent terrorist threats and attacks

electronic surveillance
using hidden microphones to secretly monitor the conversations of people

encrypted messages
messages written in code

espionage
spying

GCHQ
short for Britain's Government Communications Headquarters

hacking
unauthorised entry into a computer network or website

homeland security
efforts to prevent a terrorist attack on home soil

infiltrate
to gain access to something

informer
someone who provides information, usually top secret

intelligence
information gathered by undercover agents

Undercover agents maintain national security by protecting key members of state such as the president or prime minister.

national security
the safety of a country

surveillance
closely watching a person or a group of people

wiretapping
secretly connecting to a telephone line to listen to conversations

sabotage
the deliberate destruction or damage of something

undercover
acting in secret

GLOSSARY

Al-Qaeda
an extreme Islamic group founded by Osama Bin Laden

assassination
the organised killing of someone

cipher
a secret or disguised way of writing; a code

computer fraud
using computers to obtain information and using it to commit a crime

conquered
defeated in a war

cyber attacks
the use of computer viruses to disrupt or 'crash' a computer system

deceive
to mislead or deliberately trick someone

disloyal
not faithful or loyal, not trustworthy

enslaved
made to work as a slave

fictional
made up, not real

hieroglyphs
an ancient Egyptian form of writing with pictures

identity
a person's name, address and personal history

intercepted
captured or stopped from arriving

money laundering
a way of disguising where money obtained from criminal activities, such as drug dealing, has come from

organised crime
structured criminal groups

overthrow
the removal or downfall of a country's leader

political assassinations
killings done for political purposes

political tensions
arguments between groups with different political views

recruited
persuaded to join an organisation

regain
to take or win back something

satellite
a device in space that orbits the Earth, taking photographs or sending information as radio signals

subjects
the citizens of a country

DOUBLE AGENTS!

Spies usually operate undercover and stay out of the headlines. But sometimes they are caught, often while working for the other side. These are five of the most famous double agents.

1. SPY TURNED TV STAR

Russian citizen Anna Vasil'yevna Kushchyenko, also known as Anna Chapman, was arrested in June 2010 in New York City on suspicion of spying against the USA. Chapman and other members of her alleged spy ring pleaded guilty and were deported to Russia in July 2010 as part of a prisoner swap, with US prisoners also released and sent home. Back in Russia, Chapman soon became a popular TV star with her own show, and is even tipped for future political success!

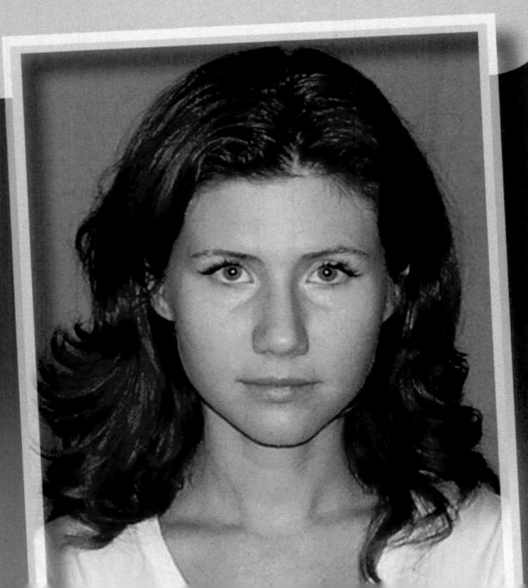

2. DANCING DOUBLE AGENT

During World War I (1914–1918), Dutch dancer Margaretha Zelle (stage name Mata Hari) was persuaded by Germany to spy for them. She passed secrets from the important politicians and generals she danced for, back to her German spymasters. But Mata Hari went too far when she offered to spy for France too, just so she could pass French secrets back to Germany. The French intercepted one of her messages, and she was sentenced to death by firing squad in 1917.

3. SPOT THE BIRDY!

In Iran, suspicious government officials arrested two pigeons in 2008 for suspected spying! The story might not be as strange as it sounds. The pigeons were discovered close to one of the country's controversial nuclear facilities. Iran's nuclear programme has been an issue with Western governments, as the West believes that Iran is developing nuclear weapons. Iranian officials suspected the birds were carrying photographic equipment and had been trained to gather evidence!

4. POISONED TEA

Former KGB agent Alexander Litvinenko escaped from Russia when the former president, Vladimir Putin, came to power. He fled to London, UK, and wrote two books accusing Putin and his supporters of 'terrorist acts'. In November 2006, while at a restaurant, Litvinenko's cup of tea was poisoned with polonium-210, a highly toxic substance. He died three weeks later. Even to this day, no one has been brought to trial for his murder.

5. SUICIDE SPY

A Jordanian doctor who had been recruited to spy for the United States turned double agent in 2009, and blew himself up on a US base. The CIA believed Humam Khalil Abu-Mulal al-Balawi had requested a meeting on the US base in Afghanistan to pass on secrets about Al-Qaeda. Instead, the Muslim militant detonated a bomb he was carrying, killing seven CIA agents.

CIPHER WHEEL

Exchange secret messages with your friends using this amazing cipher wheel to create spy codes.

You will need:

- pencil • pair of scissors
- tracing paper • card • glue
- compass • split pin

1

Trace the outer wheel shown right, including the text. Then trace the inner wheel separately. Glue the two tracings onto card. Cut out both wheels. Make sure you do not cut off the black triangle on the smaller wheel.

2

With a compass, make a small hole in the middle of both wheels. Place the small wheel on top of the big wheel, and put the split pin through the holes to make your cipher wheel.

3

Write down the message you want to send, for example, 'WE MEET AT MIDNIGHT'. Make sure you destroy the message once you have made your code!

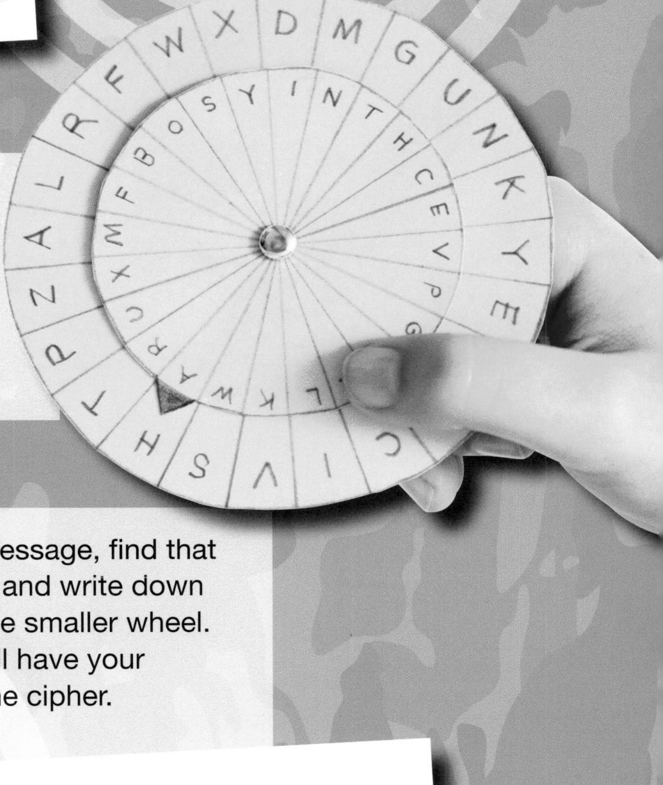

4

Choose a letter to be your 'key', for example, the letter H. Turn the smaller wheel until the black triangle points to the key.

5

Now, for each letter of your message, find that character on the outer wheel, and write down the letter that is below it on the smaller wheel. When you have finished, you'll have your encrypted message! This is the cipher.

WE MEET AT MIDNIGHT
SP NPPR MR NLICLTAR

Got it?

Your friend will need to make their own cipher wheel to decode your cipher. All they need to know is the key, in this case the letter 'H'.

GOING UNDERCOVER!

CYBER SEARCH

Start your spy investigation by visiting the website of the International Spy Museum in Washington DC, USA:
www.spymuseum.org/exhibits

FBI
Check out the official FBI website's brilliant interactive museum:
www.fbi.gov/about-us/history

MI5
Track down MI5's history archive with images dating back 100 years. Go to **www.mi5.gov.uk** and click on 'MI5 History'.

MI6
Infiltrate the MI6 website and find out fascinating facts and details:
www.sis.gov.uk

CIA
Tap into the CIA interactive museum. Go to **www.cia.gov** and click on 'CIA Museum'.

APPS & READS

Spy app allows you to turn your iPod into a secret listening device! The *Secret* app allows you to send and receive encrypted text messages and emails from your friends. Both are available on iTunes:
www.itunes.com

Try out these fantastic non-fiction reads:

Spies: Behind Enemy Lines by Jim Pipe (Wayland, 2011)

Amazing Academy: Spying by Nick Page (Make Believe Ideas, 2009)

INDEX